23.60

J636.08

DEC 31 2015

D0937021

DISCOVERING
STEM at the
Zoo

STEM in the Real World

Therese Shea

PowerKiDS press

New York

Published in 2016 by The Rosen Publishing Group, Inc.
29 East 21st Street, New York, NY 10010

Copyright © 2016 by The Rosen Publishing Group, Inc.

All rights reserved. No part of this book may be reproduced in any form without permission in writing from the publisher, except by a reviewer.

First Edition

Editor: Sarah Machajewski
Book Design: Mickey Harmon

Photo Credits: Cover (zookeeper) AFP/Stringer/Getty Images; cover, pp. 1, 3–4, 6, 8, 10, 12, 14, 16, 18, 20, 22–24 (banner design) linagifts/Shutterstock.com; cover, pp. 1, 8, 10, 18 (logo/caption box) Vjom/Shutterstock.com; p. 5 © iStockphoto.com/ Steve Zmina; p. 7 Johan Swanepoel/Shutterstock.com; p. 9 wolfmaster13/Shutterstock.com; p. 11 Norman Chan/Shutterstock.com; p. 12 SasinT/Shutterstock.com; p. 13 http://commons.wikimedia.org/wiki/File:Giants_of_the_Savanna_Inhabitants.jpg; p. 15 jeep2499/Shutterstock.com; p. 17 Taylor S. Kennedy/Getty Images; p. 19 Al Behrman/APImages.com; p. 20 (inset) jaroslava V/Shutterstock.com; p. 21 CARL COURT/Stringer/AFP/Getty Images; p. 22 Pavel L Photo and Video/Shutterstock.com.

Library of Congress Cataloging-in-Publication Data

Shea, Therese, author.
 Discovering STEM at the zoo / Therese Shea.
   pages cm. — (STEM in the real world)
 Includes bibliographical references and index.
 ISBN 978-1-4994-0928-4 (pbk.)
 ISBN 978-1-4994-0930-7 (6 pack)
 ISBN 978-1-4994-0974-1 (library binding)
 1. Zoos—Miscellanea—Juvenile literature. 2. Science—Study and teaching (Elementary)—Juvenile literature. I. Title.
 QL76.S54 2016
 590.73—dc23
                            2015009243

Manufactured in the United States of America

CPSIA Compliance Information: Batch #WS15PK: For Further Information contact Rosen Publishing, New York, New York at 1-800-237-9932

Contents

Surrounded by STEM

A day at the zoo might be the best way to learn about animals. It's surely the most fun way! Whenever you learn about animals, you're learning about science. Biology is the science that deals with all forms of life. Zoology is a kind of biology that studies animals.

The zoo is a perfect place to see STEM in action. "STEM" stands for "science, **technology**, **engineering**, and math." Zoo workers use STEM skills every day as they care for animals.

STEM Smarts

Use this smartphone screen as a tool to help you learn more about discovering STEM at the zoo.

Let's take a trip to the zoo. Zoo workers aren't the only ones who can use STEM skills here. You can, too!

What's to Eat?

Zoo workers need to know the best foods to feed each species, or kind, of animal to keep them healthy. You can't feed an alligator and an elephant the same food. Their bodies need different kinds of **nutrients**. An alligator is a carnivore, or meat eater, and an elephant is an herbivore, or plant eater.

Many zoos have a nutrition center. This is where each animal's meals are planned and where food is prepared each day. It's the zoo's kitchen!

Check out part of the yearly shopping list of the St. Louis Zoo in Missouri. Zoo workers use science to know *what to* feed the animals and math to know *how much* the "groceries" cost.

5 tons (4.5 mt) of carrots
20 tons (18 mt) of herring
7.5 tons (6.8 mt) of bananas
5.5 tons (5 mt) of apples
18 tons (16 mt) of lettuce
1.5 tons (1.4 mt) of squid
75 pounds (34 kg) of earthworms
13,000 bales of hay
1,200,000 adult crickets
1,625,000 mealworms
22,000 mice

STEM Smarts

Every animal has a special diet. At the St. Louis Zoo, it takes about 24 hours to prepare one day's worth of food for all the animals!

Nibbling Numbers

Zoo workers need to know their animals in order to know what to feed them. Workers also need to use math to figure out how much to feed them.

At the National Zoo in Washington, D.C., and Zoo Atlanta in Georgia, the giant pandas eat about 200 pounds (91 kg) of **bamboo** each day! That means the zoos have to plan ahead, using math. They know they'll need at least 73,000 pounds (33,112 kg) a year. In Washington, bamboo is grown on the zoo grounds. In Atlanta, the zoo sometimes asks people for bamboo from their backyards.

A wild giant panda eats mostly bamboo, but may eat other grasses and small animals from time to time. In zoos, giant pandas are fed bamboo, sugarcane, rice, carrots, apples, and sweet potatoes.

Habitat Design

One of the most important tasks at the zoo is making sure each animal has the best **habitat** possible. Zoo habitats must mimic, or appear to be like, an animal's natural home. Some dolphins, for example, need to swim in big pools of salt water.

Zoo habitat **designers** work to build habitats that keep animals safe, healthy, and happy. They use science to understand an animal's needs. They use technology, such as computers, to design and build habitats. They also use math to figure out how much it costs to build habitats, and how to spend the money wisely.

Red pandas love to climb and sleep in trees. Zoo habitat designers must make sure there are lots of tall trees in the red pandas' home at the zoo.

Engineering an Exhibit

Many people must work together to make the best habitat possible. Engineers work with habitat designers to plan and oversee construction of zoo **exhibits**.

To build a tiger exhibit, for example, engineers must know how high a tiger can jump. Tigers have been known to leap more than 12 feet (3.7 m)! Fences around their exhibit must be higher than this so they don't escape. Engineers use math and technology to take measurements and design an exhibit with the right features.

STEM Smarts

A zoo engineer works with an **architect** during construction. Besides building a great habitat, they need to make sure zoo visitors can safely see the animals.

The Dallas Zoo in Texas created this exhibit so that many kinds of African animals could live together peacefully.

Life Support

Life-support engineers oversee the systems that help animals survive in zoos, such as water, **temperature**, and airflow. Many species of animals come from **climates** much different from the climate of their zoo.

Take hippos, for example. They spend much of their life in the water. They're used to the warm temperatures of Africa and need their swimming water to be at least 60 degrees Fahrenheit (16 degrees Celsius). At many zoos, outside temperatures go below this. So, the hippos' water needs to heated with machines.

STEM Smarts

Even though we picture them in warm climates, big cats, such as tigers and lions, can live in the cold. However, zoologists pay attention to their behavior and the weather to see if it's okay for the cats to be outside.

Technology is used to keep hippos warm, but they have natural ways of cooling down. They cover themselves with cold water or mud!

Tools for the Job

When you think of technology, you probably think of smartphones, computers, and tablets. Technology is actually any tool that people use and the way they use it.

In a zoo, technology includes computers that are used to keep records and video cameras that are used to watch the animals. Zoo workers also use shovels, rakes, and whistles as well as two-way radios to talk to other workers. Certain animal studies may call for using **microscopes** and other scientific tools.

STEM Smarts

At least one zoo worker thinks that a hand is the best tool. "Animals see and respond to the movement of our hands," he said.

Zoo workers' tools can be quite simple!

High-Tech Energy

Some zoos are using new kinds of technology, such as solar panels. Solar panels use the sun's light to create electricity. They're a great example of engineering!

The Cincinnati Zoo in Ohio has 6,400 solar panels in its parking lot. The solar panels can power about 20 percent of the zoo's electricity. How does the zoo use electricity? It's used to heat indoor habitats, such as the gorilla house. It also powers lights, ticket machines, and more.

These solar panels cost the Cincinnati Zoo $11 million to build. However, that price tag was worth it–the zoo says the panels have helped lower its electricty bill!

Animal Math

Math is a big part of zoo life, too. Each year, the London Zoo in England measures and weighs each of its animals. That's more than 16,000 creatures! Workers compare the measurements to the measurements recorded the year before. This is one way they can tell if an animal is healthy.

It's not easy to measure some animals. Tigers are trained to stand against glass. Camels may be drawn to a scale with a treat!

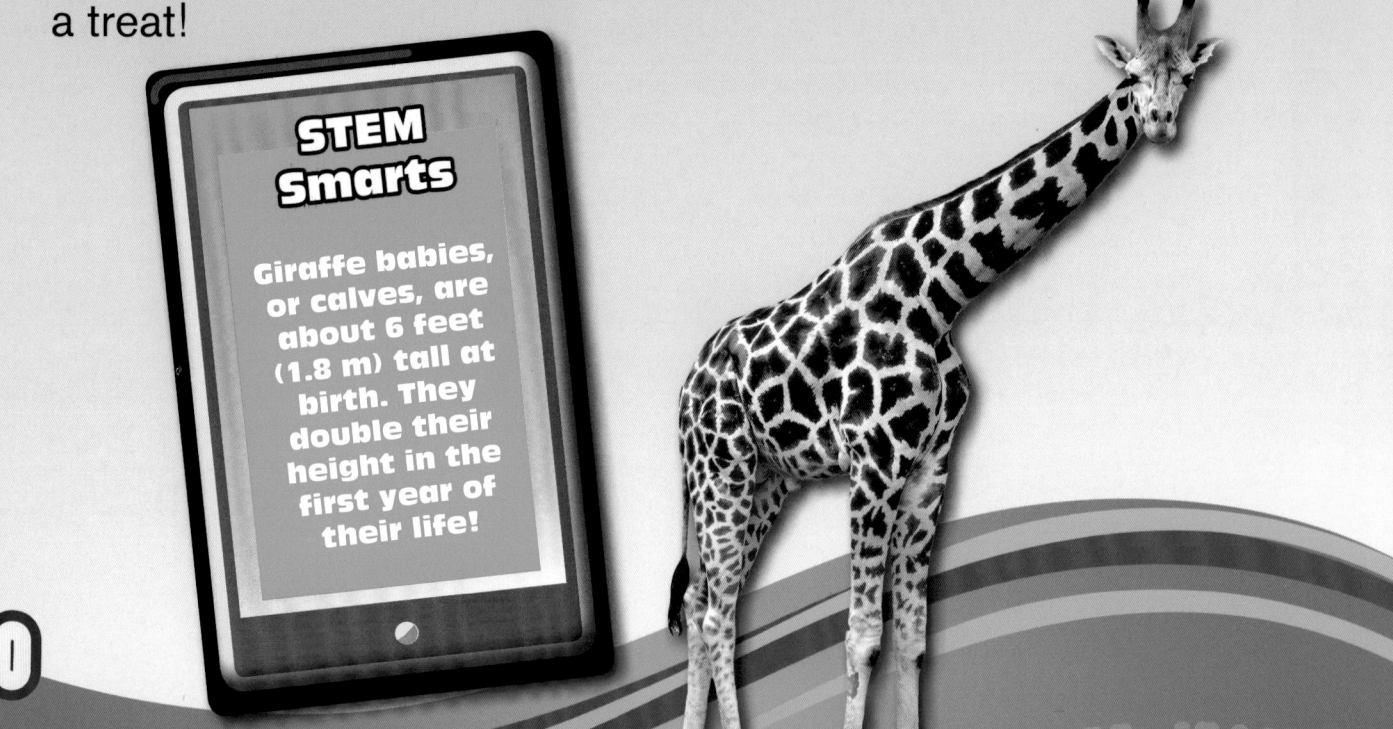

STEM Smarts

Giraffe babies, or calves, are about 6 feet (1.8 m) tall at birth. They double their height in the first year of their life!

This scale is the perfect tool for measuring tiny animals.

The Zoo Needs You!

The zoo is the perfect place to learn about STEM. If you think you'd like to spend time at a zoo using STEM skills, you might consider working in a zoo someday.

Some zoos need **volunteers**. That's a good way to find out if zoo work is for you. If it is, you can go to school to become a zoo worker. You'll take a lot of STEM classes to prepare. By thinking about STEM skills in your everyday life, you'll be a STEM pro in no time!

Glossary

architect: A person who designs buildings and may oversee their construction.

bamboo: A giant woody grass.

climate: The weather conditions in an area over a long period of time.

designer: A person who plans the workings of something before it's built.

engineering: The use of science and math to improve our world.

exhibit: A public display.

habitat: An animal or plant's natural home.

microscope: A tool used for viewing very small objects.

nutrient: Something a living thing needs to grow and stay alive.

technology: The way people do something using tools and the tools that they use.

temperature: How hot or cold something is.

volunteer: A person who does something for free.

Index

Websites

Due to the changing nature of Internet links, PowerKids Press has developed an online list of websites related to the subject of this book. This site is updated regularly. Please use this link to access the list: www.powerkidslinks.com/stem/zoo